Contents

Words appearing in the text in bold,
like this, are explained in the Glossary.

 Find out more about how things are
made at www.heinemannexplore.co.uk

What is in chocolate?

Most people enjoy eating chocolate. Chocolate contains some things that are good for your body, but eating too much chocolate can be unhealthy.

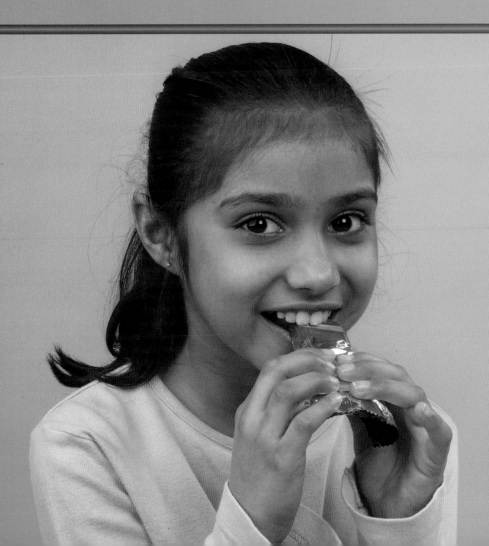

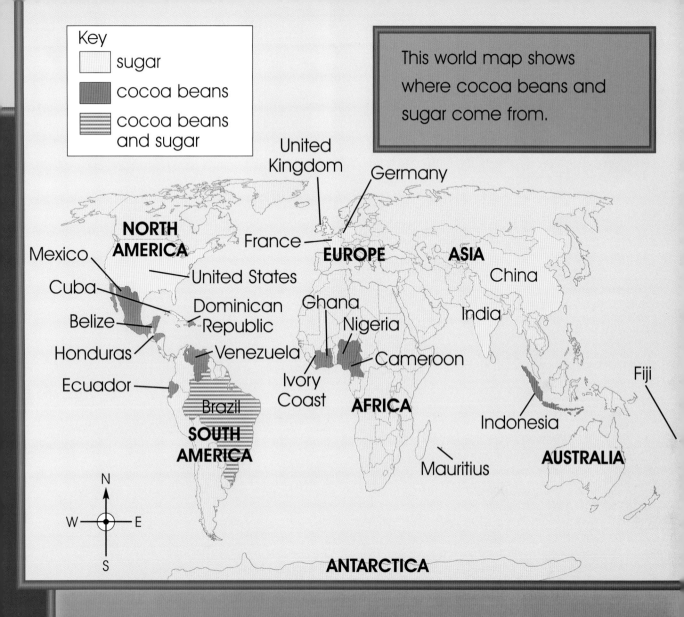

Key
- sugar
- cocoa beans
- cocoa beans and sugar

This world map shows where cocoa beans and sugar come from.

NORTH AMERICA

Mexico
Cuba
Belize
Honduras
Ecuador

United States
Dominican Republic
Venezuela
Brazil

SOUTH AMERICA

United Kingdom
Germany
France
EUROPE

Ghana
Nigeria
Ivory Coast
Cameroon
AFRICA

Mauritius

ASIA
China
India

Indonesia

AUSTRALIA

Fiji

N
W — E
S

ANTARCTICA

Chocolate is made from **cocoa beans**.
Chocolate also contains milk and sugar.
These **ingredients** come from many different parts of the world.

5

Who makes chocolate bars?

Several different **companies** make chocolate bars. Each company has one or more factories where the chocolate is made. Many people work for a chocolate company.

Some people work the machines in the chocolate factory. Other people pack the chocolate into boxes. Some make up names for the bars and **design** the wrappers.

This man's job is to check that the chocolate tastes good.

Cocoa beans

Cocoa beans grow in pods on cocoa trees. When the pods are **ripe**, the farmers cut them from the tree and take out the beans.

Workers spread out the beans in the sun
to dry. They pack the dried beans into
large bags. Then they send the beans
to local companies. They send the
beans to the chocolate **company**.

Sugar

Cocoa beans are very bitter. Lots of sugar is needed to make the chocolate taste sweet. Sugar is made from stalks of **sugar cane** or from **sugar beet**.

These stalks of sugar cane are cut by workers in Brazil.

Sugar cane is fed into machines. The machines squeeze out the sugary juice. The juice is then boiled until it turns into small **crystals** of sugar.

Milk

Cows make the milk that is used in chocolate. Milking machines suck the milk from the cows into pipes.

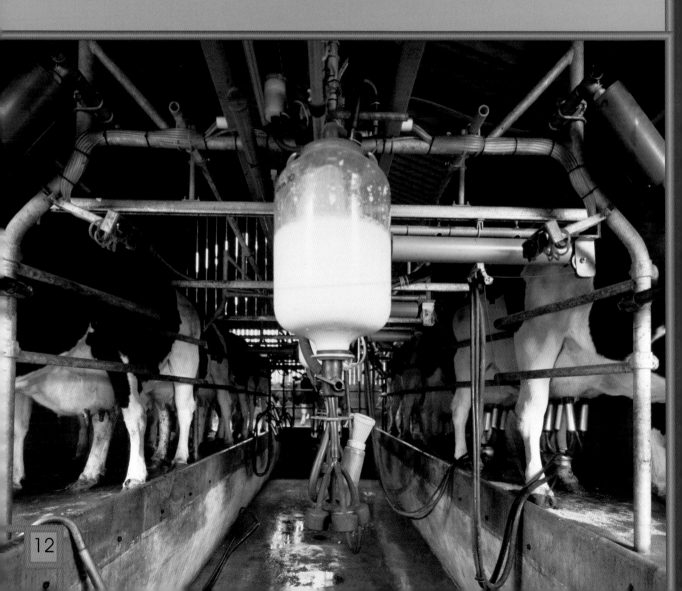

Once the milk is at the creamery, it is heated to kill any **germs**.

The milk is stored in a **refrigerator tank**. A milk tanker takes the milk to a **creamery**. A machine dries some of the milk.

Other ingredients

Many chocolate bars contain other **ingredients**. Flavourings, such as fruit and caramel, give some bars a particular taste.

peanuts

coconut

caramel

Peanuts, rice crisps, almonds, or other nuts are often mixed into the chocolate. Some chocolate bars are filled with coconut or crunchy biscuit.

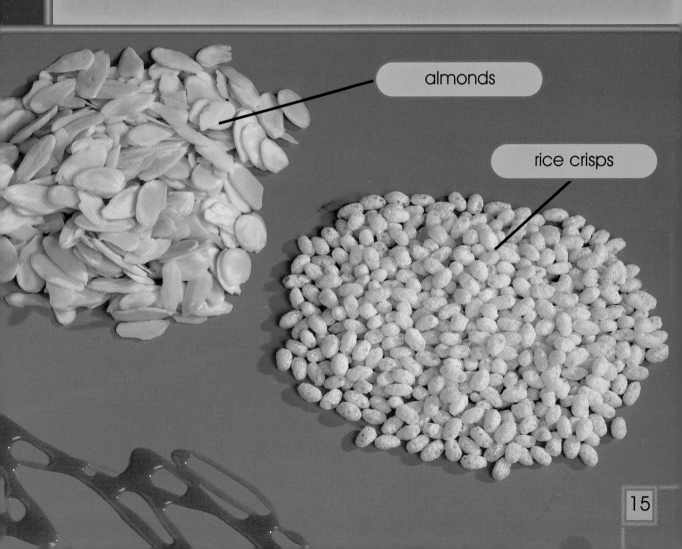

almonds

rice crisps

Preparing the cocoa beans

Ships and lorries take **cocoa beans**, sugar, and dried milk to the chocolate factory. Here machines clean the cocoa beans. They take off the shells.

The beans are slowly roasted in a machine.

The ground beans turn into a solid called cocoa mass.

Workers feed the roasted beans into a machine called a grinder. It grinds the hot beans into small pieces. The ground beans are then cooled.

Mixing in sugar and milk

Sugar and milk powder are mixed into the cocoa mass to make a soft dough. The dough moves through rollers. They squash it into a fine powder.

The mixture is heated to change it into a liquid. The liquid is stirred for twelve hours.

The liquid now smells very chocolatey!

Bars of chocolate

While the chocolate mixture is still hot, it pours from the trough into **moulds**. Each mould is the shape of a single chocolate bar.

These moulds have **ridges** to divide the chocolate into chunks.

The moulds move through a **refrigerator**.
As the chocolate cools, it changes into a
solid. Then the moulds are taken off. Now
you can see the bars of chocolate!

Chocolate wrappers

The bars of solid milk chocolate move along a **conveyor belt**. A machine puts a wrapper around each bar.

The wrapper keeps out the air and keeps the chocolate fresh.

The bars of chocolate are then packed into boxes. Each box contains the same kind of chocolate bar.

Storing the chocolate

Lorries take the boxes of chocolate bars to a **warehouse**. The warehouse is always kept at the same cool temperature. This stops the chocolate from melting.

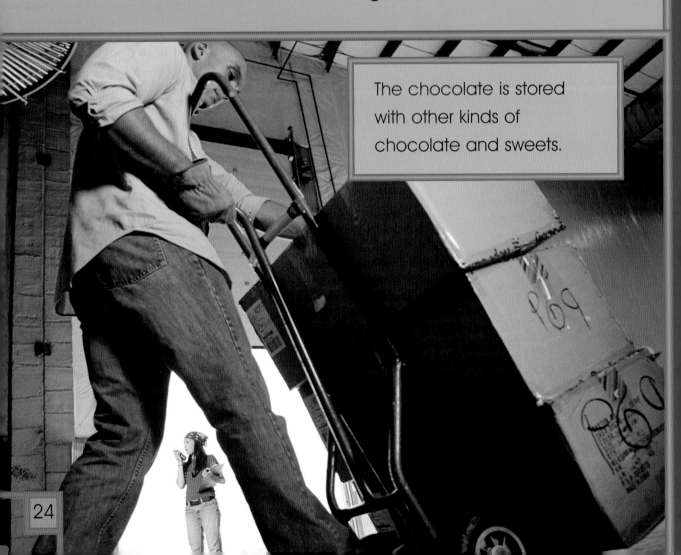

The chocolate is stored with other kinds of chocolate and sweets.

When a shop needs some more
chocolate bars to sell, they order them
from the warehouse. A lorry takes boxes
of chocolate bars to the shop.

Selling the chocolate bars

Many kinds of shops sell chocolate bars. The shopkeeper stacks them on racks so that you can choose the kind of chocolate bar you want.

The shopkeeper pays the chocolate **company** for the bars. The chocolate company uses the money to pay its workers, and to make more chocolate bars.

Some of the money you pay for a bar of chocolate goes to the chocolate company.

From start to finish

Cocoa beans are cleaned, roasted, and ground.

Different cocoa ingredients are mixed with sugar and milk products.

The mixture is heated to make it liquid.

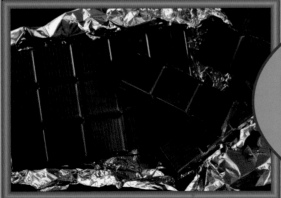

The liquid is poured into **moulds** and cooled to make bars of chocolate.

A closer look

A chocolate bar wrapper tells you about the **ingredients** in the chocolate bar.

STORE IN A COOL DRY PLACE

Ingredients: sugar, Fairtrade cocoa butter, dried cream whole milk powder, Fairtade cocoa mass, cocoa mass, emulsifier: soya lecithin (non GM), real vanilla.
Cocoa solids: minimum 28%.
Milk solids: minimum 20%
Fairtrade ingredients 24%

MAY CONTAIN TRACES OF NUTS ~~AND WHEAT~~

Ingredients

NUTRITION INFORMATION PER

Energy	2260kj/541kcal
Protein	6.6g
Carbohydrate	57.7g
Fat	31.5g

Glossary

bitter not sweet

cocoa bean seed of the cocoa plant

company group of people who work together

conveyor belt machine that carries things on a long loop from one place to another

creamery factory that makes things from milk, such as butter, cheese, and powdered milk

crystal clear, solid piece

design decide how something will look

germ tiny living thing that can make you ill

ingredients things that are mixed together to make something

mould hollow container

refrigerator tank or large container that is kept cool

ridge narrow strip that is higher than the surface around it

ripe when seeds are ready to fall off the plant

sugar beet plant whose roots can be used to make sugar

sugar cane plant whose stem can be used to make sugar

warehouse building where things are stored

Places to visit

Cadbury World, Birmingham: museum devoted to
Cadbury's chocolate, but you must book your visit
in advance.

Websites:

www.bccca.org.uk
This website has information about ingredients and
sustainable cocoa growing.

www.barry-callebaut.com
This website contains a history of chocolate and an
explanation of how chocolate is made.

www.cadburylearingzone.co.uk
This website includes information on what life was like in
a chocolate factory 100 years ago.

www.cocoatree.org
This website gives information about cocoa farming,
including what life is like on a cocoa farm.

Index